Blackheart Hideaway

M. Lauren

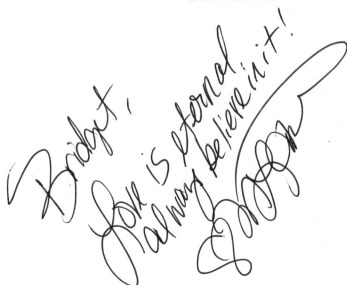

Published by MMR! Publishing Co.
Cleveland, Ohio

ISBN: 1983598046
ISBN-13: 978-1983598043

To every little black girl with a dream…

CONTENTS

SERENDIPITOUS THOUGHTS

PROSE & STREAMS OF CONSCIOUSNESS

POETRY

SHORTS

ACKNOWLEDGEMENTS

SERENDIPITOUS
THOUGHTS

JUST THOUGHTS ON LOVE

If you ask me…

Love does not have a gender or sexuality. It is simply an entity in and of itself which holds us captive. Its hold is so strong, it is inescapable. Love has no age and is not limited by time. It simply exists for whoever is willing. It lives everywhere taking up space; whether invited or not. Love is a moment or sets of moments that overtake the soul. Love is the gentle grace of a woman's gait. And the warm strength of a man's arms. It is at once joy and revelation. And, let's be clear, love does not hurt or bring pain. It may reveal but it does not overexpose you. It is simply content to wait. The verse is true: love is certainly patient and kind. It does not get jealous or boast. Love stands in the doorway and watches over those who yield to it. It is protective, perfect and fine. Love is a calm in the storm and the bringer of new life. Love simply is and always will be … hovering in the shadows awaiting those who will choose it over all.

THE MAGIC OF BLACK GIRLS

You smile so bright although the demons stay at your back.
You keep pushing, sis, knowing your enemies have come to attack.
You don't run even when your legs want to give way.
You never hide but if it hurts you won't stay.
You live each day ready to face a new void.
You could jump over or fall in, but you make your own choice.
With your heart on your sleeve, skin shining, your spirit free.
You rise above all, effortlessly.
You take no shit and hold no bars.
You are the one that calls the shots, the one who loves all.
You are a woman, a sovereign queen.
Black girl, sugar, spice bronze goddess and everything in between.

PROSE & STREAMS OF CONSCIOUSNESS

THE FIRST THREE MONTHS

The first three months of our love affair was pure passion. Makeout sessions against the wall; light switch digging into my back. Stopping in traffic in the throes of a deep, never-ending kiss. Only parting lips at the barrage of irritable car horns behind us. Squeaking bed springs every night detailing the experimentation of new tastes and feelings and positions. Doing things we had never done with anyone else, reveling in the novelty of the newness all the while falling in love with each glance.

First dates turned into first kisses became the first time in the first week and a first love within the first month of a first-time love affair. Keys opening doors of homes that don't belong to the other. A stashed sweater here, a stored toothbrush there. Moving much too rapidly but unable to see the break in the road before us. Caught up in straddling on chairs, recreating scenes from classic black cinema and stretching out the crook in my neck from nights spent using hard abs as my pillow. Restless without each other, finding comfort in spending every possible waking moment together. When they see me alone they ask, "Where is he?" and they never see you without me in your eyes. Stopping on the street to watch me walk as you take me in every time like the first time; newness ringing through our rapid comfort.

We know each other too well but all the while not well enough.

Feeding you breakfast at night, camping out on the floor devouring chicken and rice before we push plates to the side in the urgency to feel your heaviness smother me with light kisses. A husky, "Come here," hips swinging as wanting eyes rove, a meeting of lips causing mental collapse. Whispering secrets until night meets day, forgetting half of what you said as a nap date turns into teasing touches with the television glowing in the background. Blue light shining on my face as you watch me sleep, turned off by your cinematic preferences but never by you. Holding hands up to lips in dark theaters, giggling at the envy of everyone around us wishing they had what we had.

Grabbing your hand as we pass boutiques with clothes you imagine you'll buy for me but never get the chance because our whirlwind will come to a finite stop like all tornados do.

Three months of satiated bliss blanketed with early adorations and steamy glances. Covered in chocolate, wine, grapes in the living room; sweating and panting on the floor. A love undiscovered, unmarred by bitterness. We crammed like, lust, love into 131,487 minutes. If only we had a dollar for every minute we could still never be as rich as our enchantment. A love that would never grow but could never be forgotten. Cherished always in the pit of my heart, taking up space to be rented by the next 90-day amorous binge. A love I'll always search for. Never to be found again. Never to replicate itself. And always leave me craving it once again. Until true love rescues me from its hold. Until then ... the memories.

STAY AWHILE

It's been some time... Since I last kissed you hugged you felt you saw you missed you needed you... Glad you're back even if only for a minutes blink... You walked in and I wanted to rip your clothes off but I need to take you in one sip at a time savor you one bite at a time be patient it would come... But first sit let me take your coat... Hungry? Let's eat show me that I've missed… a gentle touch on the nape of my neck you watch me you missed me needed me glad you're back gently touching my collarbone as you lean in gentle kiss on my cheek let me feel your lips on mine baby... baby I want you slow down let's take our time.

Where have you been? Is Europe beautiful in summer? What did you do there? Did you bring pictures? You missed me? You thought of me at night? You drank wine for me that tasted like melon suckle from my lips? You brought me things? Chocolates and books? You wished I was with you? Crisp cool white sheets against my honey kissed brown? You missed me? Lips on my fingertips, heart flutters, don't leave me again.

Why must you go?

Every time you leave you take my heart, I don't want it back. Kiss me again give me melon suckle wine kisses from temple to toe. Want to see what you've missed? Just open your eyes don't leave me again. Blend your dark chocolate with my toffee confections. Give me I miss yous with every touch give me I need yous with every look.

Tempt me for I will surely fall watch as they crumble baby take down my walls. Surrender to me if you missed me like you say and I will submit to your touch as I've needed you today, today, today you are back home don't leave me again. Or take me with you as you've stolen my heart. Don't ransack my love any longer. Why do you rise? Baby come back I'm not done missing you he said okay, I'll stay awhile.

TELLING HIM

He asked me why I couldn't sleep. He was wondering why all my midnights were spent moaning through tossing and turning. He asked me how come I rested with a smile on my face and my eyes fluttered so much at night. He was curious as to why I couldn't seem to get any of my thoughts straight or why I always appeared flustered when I woke up in the middle of the night.

He wasn't so sure of why I chose a berry-hued lipstick all of the sudden and topped it with the shiniest gloss I could possibly muster. He didn't understand why I started wearing more than brown eyeliner and brow pencil and he thought maybe I was trying to make him see me differently. He was thinking that I was thinking that he wasn't seeing me as sexy anymore and I wanted to vamp it up to get his attention. He said I got it. He said I didn't need makeup and squats and all those hip-revealing stretch denims. He said no matter what changed, he still found me sexy and attractive and "hell, I could eat you right now." But I declined. Told him I didn't feel like it.

I didn't tell him that my panties still held remnants of the afternoon encounter that was the whole reason I had worn a skirt in the first place. He didn't need to know that I used your face as a balance beam on my lunch break and had finally deemed his lips useless at 12:02pm. He really didn't have to know that I had a bright red fist imprinted on my left thigh and four short scratches under the cup of my ass. He didn't need to know that I begged for your body in secret codes via email at 8:02am and at 8:05 you were locking the door to my office for an "important meeting" that left me panting, heaving and teased.

I didn't think it would be a good idea to let him know that I ignored his usual morning text because I was fanning myself at 8:23am and checking my neck for bite marks. That I had to attempt rebuttoning my blouse three times because my hands shook in anticipation of lunch … that you had taken less than 20 minutes to break me down and take the last of my strength.

Why should I tell him that I had spent the last 8 months of my 40 hours a week ogling you? Making small talk. Checking your ring finger for tan lines. Taking up your proposal for outdoor lunch. Talking about my distaste for those romantic comedies he insists on dragging me to. Dreaming about you after the first time you touched the small of my back as we entered the building after that long, boring training. Touching my lips after the first time you kissed me; after work, next to my car, in the dark garage. Touching myself in the shower wishing I could've taken you there under the concrete beams.

He doesn't need to know how many nights I spent awake texting you while he dozed off until the sunlight. Can't tell him how you never failed to get my coffee order right even though he thought I was "more of a tea girl." I'll keep to myself how I felt the first time that an anonymous bouquet appeared on my desk – lilies surrounding a single white rose – your signature. He can't ever know how you teased me with illicit photos to the email I made specifically for you and how I only bought expensive lace so that I could tease you back. He'll never understand how I craved you from the moment you stepped off the 9th floor elevator and stumbled into my office, lost.

I cannot tell him that in my dreams you'd seduced me before I had a chance to learn your full name. That after you told me your first name and I repeated it, it tasted like honey and cinnamon on the tip of my tongue. That I contemplated switching jobs to get closer to you but you ended that before the thought had a chance to form. That day you finally came back down to my floor, rushed past the administrative assistant and barged right into my office without so much as a glance toward my gawking coworkers. I won't tell him how you lifted me from my chair, sat me on the desk and snatched my head back, hair wrapped around your hand. Parted my lips with yours, kissed me with rawness, roughness, desire ...

How I whispered your name there in my office ...

...Gianna

POETRY

M. Lauren

HIDEAWAY

Hideaway

Here in me

Deep inside my depths

Find rest

Comfort

My love

Hideaway

Here with me

Release your burdens

Find calm

Safety

My love

Hideaway

Here beyond me

Sustain your heart

Lock it away

Find shelter

Home

Here in me

DARKNESS

God must have painted you with midnight
The way your skin glows
Warm under my fingertips
He must have seen the deepest night
And thought of you
The way your skin lays
Smooth across your bones
Blanketing each feature
God must have known
That I needed your mahogany in my life
And created you
Just for me
To stroke my finger upon your flesh
Like brush to canvas
A scene of languid love at nighttime
He must have gathered up darkness
And injected it into your being
So that I could marvel at your beauty
Shooing gawkers away with my scowl
So that I can keep you to myself
A masterpiece molded at midnight by God, Himself

THE WORLD

When I ruled the world
I molded his clay with my hands
And shaped his mind in my sideways glance
I opened his eyes with cool breath on his cheek
And my obnoxious laugh
It made his heart beat

When I ruled the world
I took in his form with my eyes
And played around the images in my mind
I let go and let my plan devise

When I ruled the world
He was the king of my land
He reigned over my body
And my heart lay in the palm of his hand

When I ruled the world
We took over the night
He grew wings and my black knight
Took off in an armored flight

When I ruled the world
I was his damsel to tame
At daybreak he left me and at night fall
He came
Stringing along tales and sporting game
He nourished my soul
With an uncontainable love
My hunger he fed
And my thirst he quenched
With just one look
I knew everything he meant

When I ruled the world
They came like thieves in the night
Tied, shackled and bound my king

Blurred and erased my sight

When I ruled the world
The past I now live
A queen dethroned
No more, no less, no passion to give
I once ruled the world
They claim it a dream
I travel endlessly through this hell
Searching for my king
We shall rule yet again

Exacting

ruthless

revenge

WHAT IS A KISS?

the sweetest I love you
silent passion unrelenting
an intimate embrace
that says it all
tender I missed yous
desperate don't ever leaves
sultry I want yous
decadent you want mes
a nervous goodnight
a hopeful come closer
a sensual come hither
a longing stay awhile
muting a lover's moan
encouraging one to let loose
reassurance in doubt
a pondering will I see you again?
A naughty one night invitation
a fiery lead on
an innocent flirtation
first time touches
and everlasting promises
secret rendezvous
jealousy rising
resolutions and changes of heart
everything you wanted
but couldn't say
every night you wanted
but couldn't stay
every thought
every feeling
every word
every kiss between lovers

FOR YOU

I put a photo of us on the mantelpiece

In our home

That we have yet to share

I make up the king-sized bed

With sheets soft and scented light

The way I imagine you would like it

I use lemon scented cleanser

Cause I know you enjoy citrus

I douse myself in the scents of summer

Because you like it when I smell like happiness

I show my legs when we go out

But I never wear clothes when we're in

I dream about our children

I name them in my diary

I keep secrets of how I feel for you

Even though I know you feel the same

I close my eyes

Just so I can see myself in a white dress

Taking your last name

I come when you call

I never leave you waiting long

I listen for your car to pull up

The minute you leave your place

My heart beats when I see you

Even if you're just walking from the kitchen to the bedroom

I keep your favorite foods around

I always will

I listen to your music

And watch your favorite shows

I get pretty for you to lie on the couch

But I can no longer sleep if I'm alone

I write poetry about you

Then I notice you looking over my shoulder

And when I look in your eyes

I see love come alive

For each word that I've written

A kiss

A smile

A hand through my curls

For each line that you are mentioned

You tell me I am your love

Your one

Your world

For every poem ended

With you in mind

You sing my praises in new ways

I write my love for you

Because you love me always

RHYME

I tried to write you a rhyme
to tell the world how I feel about you
a rhyme that would scream from the pages
I love you

so I put pen to paper
and the words would not come
so I scrapped that
opened my mouth

but

still no words
I tried to write you a rhyme for all the times
all the smiles
all the love

I picked up the pen again
I wanted to tell the world about you
head to toe hair to skin

I wanted each word to be you
each letter a cell
it's you I cannot fail

I wanted to write you a rhyme
a syncopation a beat
a love story a poem
for you are poetry

so I hugged you in parentheses
and I caressed you with question marks
comma'd you with kisses
that a period would not stop
titillated your senses with each word I would bring
putting pen to paper
a gift to a king

all I need is an

a e i o you

a formulation of letters to become words
and sentences
an everlasting rhyme to open your senses
but write I could not
thinking, I could do

so I put the pen down
to think about me and you
all I ever wanted from
my sweet king supreme
to become one

I kept thinking
like when a pen meets paper
and the result is a poem
and

you

are

poetry

so instead of that rhyme

I opened my notebook
there you are
regal against white sheets
black, bold, staring back at me

I read and reread you
write and recite you

I learned you
I remember
the words in the book

I cannot write you a rhyme
for you are rhyme itself

I breathe you I read you
then I put my notebook
back on its shelf

LOVE'S CALL

Love must have called your name

        the answer must have been sweet

by the look in your eyes

by the warmth in your smile

by the lingering in your kiss

           your answer clear

by the sweltering gaze

by the never-ending embrace

by the longing upon your lips

your response was sure

         you answered love's call

an unwavering choice

         you answered love's call

standing tall and sure

one time, truly, mine

                  you chose me

WITH YOU | WITH HIM

When I am with you
Laughter comes easy
Like rainwater in spring

When I am with him
I grin from ear to ear
Unstoppable

When I am with you
I feel alive
Young
Free

When I am with him
I am intelligent
Powerful
Otherworldly

When I am with you
My hands cannot let go
I've got to touch
Rub
Caress
Let me know that you're real

When I am with him
He lets my spirit soar
My mind connects with his

Still I am unable to let go

When I am with you
We are easy and light
Anything goes
I am complete with your body pressed against mine

When I am with him

The words flow like a rushing river
Syllables caress my temple
Sentences slide down my backside
Questions burn on my tongue

When I am with you
I glide through the air
On your nimble tongue
Your fingers slide down my back
Because of you I am undone

When I am with him
My soul stirs with new light
His hands on my hip
And lips on my shoulder
Shakes up all that you've done right

When I am with you
We are whole
Body and feeling

When I am with him
My mind
My soul
My spirit
are
Willing

When I am with you
I am satiated, satisfied

When I am with him
I am fulfilled
Complete
Daring

When I am with you
I say the unthinkable

When I am with him
I do the unreachable

When I am with you
Love rises to the tip of my heart

When I am with him
Love lives in the midst of my being

When I am with you
I am dancing on the edge of passion and hope

When I am with him
I am still
Submerged in the essence of love

When I am with you
His soul lingers on my fingertips

I am present to bask with you

But I am always with him

1,000 POEMS

I can't keep writing you poems
Every time I encounter your soft lips
On my flesh
For, if I had it my way
I would have written one thousand poems already

One thousand words describing the tingles that roll down my
spine

One thousand letters that answer the question of why I cannot
stay away

One thousand stanzas that breathe life into the memory of your
kiss

One thousand poems that tell the world of my inability to resist

I would write a poem for every minute that we've spent
Held so close our skin melds into one long stretch of brown

I would write a poem for every flick of your tongue
Creating tremors
Eliciting otherworldly moans
Writing your own erotic iambic pentameters on my back

I would write a poem for every bite
Every lick
Every suck
Every inch of unignored flesh

I would write a poem for every drip drop of sweat
Every bitten lip

Every salacious whispered thing

I would write a poem for every midnight
Turning to midday
Spent upon foam and coil
Wrapped tight
Cocoon
With you

I would write you one thousand poems

Just one will not do

YOUR HEART

I wish I could reach back
and grab my thoughts from you
sweet regrets rest on my lips
like morning dew
speaking words I'd hope were untrue
underlying quiet changes my thoughts of you
just for the moment it's me and you
can't smell the rain
for the clouds in my view
taking over my senses
I retract every thought of us
know it's for today
wont last
can't explain what came over us
want to relive the future moments we long to see
experience what's taken control of me
realizing one day this will be over and done
wishing that our secrets could carry on
carry over into something
sweeter than our lovemaking
giving ourselves to each other
our love up for the taking
yearning to reach a heavenly abyss
overstepping boundaries with every single kiss
craving for a moment to last like this
hoping that we could stay
pray maybe even die like this
wonder if we'll ever know each other
in our pasts we'll miss
wonder how we keep checking marks off on our lists
I'm everything you want
you're all I deserve

why can't we keep the flame burning
let our flesh melt in this fire?
Wait to erupt and be with you on this pyre
can't stop the music
tell me your soul is for hire?
You know that I'm the one
but the song has gone cold
started before we finished
nothing left but our souls
they intertwine in darkness
for the next life
screaming at our hearts
to make this love right
craving for the touch
when your hand meets my face
needing to feel pleased
hoping to feel safe
yelling for the control
that we lost in our minds
knowing your heart belongs to me
in your hand, you hold mine
afraid to let go
move beyond our passion
to embark on a love song
true, everlasting
holding onto the truth
suffocating the lies
your heart belongs to me
in your hand you hold mine

(in his journal) WORDS FOR JONATHAN

one day long
mesmerization grows
like lilies in clean soil
questions answered by
the look in your eye
fear erased with each passing moment
open to the what, when & howevers
we can offer

day by day
ramblings, wanderings
clumsy, careless
learning our way around each other
lingering & fumbling our way
towards familiarity
know me through kiss
two souls dancing at twilight
connected by black ink
permanent on parchment

NOTHING

Nothing

there is Nothing
no piece of artwork
no poem that I could write
nothing that could tell the world
how far you've reached
deep down to my core
to interrupt my most meaningful thought
to invade my most treasured feeling

there is Nothing
no song nor sculpted piece of fragile glass
that could express the beauty in you
the allure of your mind
the charm of your smile
could not be mimicked by watercolor
nor pounding hammer to metal
no stanza or bar
no graceful dance

Nothing

there is Nothing
no blaring instrument
or soulful orchestra
that could tell the truth of my love
how I see no one else
and think of only you

there is Nothing
no photograph or sonnet
that could capture your grace
or still the heavy breaths
when I touch you

there is Nothing

Nothing
no writing no painting
no art
you are beauty
you are style
you are grace
you are love personified

there is Nothing

only You

TO LOVE A POET

It may be neurotic
But I find it erotic

How deeply you go
Your words through my soul

Your tongue pressed against my temple
Does much

But nothing
Like your words on my mental

Your fingertips graze my skin
I feel your heartbeat from within

Waves crash against steel
Emotions rush

But nothing like

The way your work
Makes me feel

Your words invite me to other worlds
Otherwise unknown

Not yet shaped
Unconsumed with life

You fill me

With the stroke
Of your pen

The strength of 10,000 men
Against my back you push

But nothing
Like the weight of your words
Blowing breeze across my face

Your lips
Invite me for succulent tastes

I lean in to listen closer
Envelop me with your art

You watch my lips
My legs
My mind
Part

Part ways with my senses

I lose myself in your work
You work me from the outside

In

Deep inside you touch
What can never be reached

My mind and body climax simultaneously
Erupt

Leave you sticky with the residue of my love

My mind reaches out for you
My body spent

I cannot get enough
I need your tongue

I need your hands
I need your words

Take over my mind

Capture my soul
With your piece

Give me love
Then steal it away

Just as I come close
Take me back to the edge

Leave me in suspense
Leave me breathless

Then draw me in again
Take all that I have

Write it up and leave me for good

Do not return, baby
Unless you plan to come with your pen

CAPTIVE

I want to live inside his mind
Attach myself to the crevices that create who he is

And who I will become
I don't want to be one with him

I want to be him

Feel what he feels when he moves
Guide my way through his imagination
And see what he sees

I want to live inside the deepest part of his being
Come into his soul and live there for eternity
I do not want to own him

But he is mine

I do not want him as my property
But I want to possess him
In the way that he cannot move without me

He cannot think without me
His footsteps become my own

His fingertips brush my skin
And I feel it from the inside out

Let me dwell here
In the darkest pit of you

Let me navigate through the muck

Dirty up my clothing, my hair, my skin

Give me the secrets you hold captive

Deep

Within

You

I shall reside
I come to live there

You cannot escape me
You cannot run or hide

I am you

and

You are I

As I come to overtake your being
You ease your way into mine

You walk barefoot on the folds of my brain
And try to take control

But I will not move
I will not go

I will not stop
I will live forever in a place that surrenders your full control

While you plan a takeover
You have already been enslaved

There is no release
There is no escape

I have taken over
I have come to stay forever

You see me in your mirror
I captivate you one glance at a time

I will live here in you always

And you still cannot understand
How you came to be mine

SHORTS

UNLIKE ANY OTHER MAN

PART I

I've never met a man like him before. All of the assholes that I've gotten to know over the last 10 or so years; they could never even compare. I'm used to the guys who fuck up and don't even bother to offer an excuse, let alone try to rectify the problems that they caused. I'm used to meeting guys whose first question pertains to the color of my panties or even worse. I'm used to the type of guys whose number one priority is themselves and how they can get themselves as much sex as possible without even one thought about the women they are involving themselves and their penises with. I am so used to dealing with the bastards and jerks and assholes and despicables of the world that I had pretty much given up on dealing with guys period. I had pretty much said that I quit I was out of the dating game and I would rather just be alone than deal with the stupidity that these trash ass guys have to offer. But something changed.

I wasn't trying to date. I wasn't trying to meet anyone. I wasn't trying to be involved. I wasn't trying to do anything except live my life and mind my own business. But out of the hell of nowhere he showed up and started being all the things that all those other guys were not, would never and probably could never be. He was sweet, he was fun, he was funny, he was trying. When he messed up, he admitted it. When he was wrong, he apologized. When he wanted to see me, he told me. He asked me out and he called me. He took me places and he did things that I wanted to do. He exposed me to the things that he loved and he was willing to see all the things that I cherished.

Falling in love with him was easy. I knew, when I was able to tell him my secrets. When I was able to share my weirdest dreams and goals with him that everyone else scoffed at. When he wondered about my family and friends and work and my goals and the things that made me tick. When he asked me questions that didn't pertain to sexing me but spent time really getting to know how my mind works. When I was able to stop worrying about whether I'd done or said the right thing or whether or not the question I'd asked would push him away. When I was able to say how I really felt and knew he could disagree without arguing. When he took the crazy things I said to him in stride and I wasn't afraid that he'd stop dating me because of them. When we were both able to take our time with each other, putting off physical pleasure to know each other spiritually. When he asked me to come to church with him. When he invited me to family dinner and when he never let his friends say anything bad about me. When he was able to admit truths to me and I found myself able to forgive. I knew it was going to be.

When he knelt down and asked me to pray with him, I knew I could love him.

I never questioned whether he could or would love me because I knew from the beginning that it was all possible. But I questioned some things. Where did he come from and why did it take so long to get here? Why hadn't things worked like this the other times we'd tried doing this before? Why did I have to exercise so much patience and move by the hour hand when I already knew things would work out and plus, I'm a minute hand kind of girl anyway. Why… why? I asked so many whys and a few whens and a smattering of hows but one day I just woke up and realized that there would always be questions and I didn't need the answers to any of them.

I started asking myself why did it matter what the answers were and allowed myself to just feel and move through the motions of learning to love a man with the purity of love that I'd given away freely so many times before. And one day, while I was just reveling in my own feelings of newness and joy, I realized that he had many whys. And still, he was here and unlike any man I'd ever met.

UNLIKE ANY OTHER MAN

PART II

Expectations. That's what everyone told me I should let go of. Told me that expectations are the things that get in the way of finding something real and true. I've been told time and again that expectations are just a synonym for disappointment, which couldn't possibly be true. But, what they say is that expectations lead to high hopes and high hopes end in disappointment. Now, I will never be a liar and say that I've never been disappointed by someone else or even my own lofty dreams. However, I would be a fool not to expect ...

Something wonderful, beautiful ... miraculous, even.

I've spent most of my adult years alone and every time I've thought "this is it, he's the one," I've been wrong, wrong, so wrong. But this time...

There was something different. A change in the way I spoke to him. A difference in the manner in which he handled me. He was ...

Let me tell you about him ...

He was the kind of man that would wake up early, early in the morning to make sure that he had you on the phone before your morning commute just to tell you "have a good day."

He was the kind of man that slept over on Friday nights so he could cook you breakfast on Saturday afternoon.

He was the kind of man who could touch your cheek with his palm and even a sweet peck on the lips would send your head swirling into Tuesday.

He was the type of man that would ease your shoes off – left first, then right – and ease his thumbs down from your toe to your arch to your heel and back up again before you even got the chance to whisper, "My feet are killing me."

He was the type of man who anticipated your every need before you yourself had realized you needed it.

He was the type of man who would call and say, "Baby, be dressed in something pretty by 6, I'm coming to get you," and would spin you around town on his arm until the sun rose back up again.

He was the kind of man that made every woman swoon from his romance, his elegance, his fragrance …

His grandeur, his stature and dare I say it, his swagger…

He would have your mind twirling in a maze of exhilaration at the sound of his voice calling out for you to, "Please come sit closer to me."

He would give just one look and melt away all doubts, one touch would cure any ailment.

He was the kind of man that women – that I – prayed for, hoped upon, dreamed of and fantasized about.

His pure essence exuded love and reverence.

And he was the man I had high hopes and higher expectations of.

People thought that I was crazy to expect him to give me more than a few caresses before he tried to pull me into his boudoir. They said I wouldn't get anything out of him except a joyride in his California King and if I even thought of being prim and proper, he'd send me off without so much as a wave goodbye.

I don't know who they thought he was and I don't know who I imagined him to be. But, we were all wrong.

While I was waiting for him to politely usher me off to wherever the innocent girls are sent to, they assumed I was oohing and aahing until my throat became hoarse all over his loft.

Whatever they'd said about him, he did the opposite. Whenever I turned my head to catch him soaking in dirt, he'd be clean on the other side. He was pure.

I gave him months to show his true colors. And what a myriad of hues did he have for me to peek at. While all the others were holding their carefully trained breaths trying to ensure a stay for me at the Joyless Inn, he was exceeding every exaggerated hope I'd ever had the nerve to give to him.

He is everything.

Sweet and kind and funny and gentle; a gentleman makes me melt with his conversation.

I gave him a chance when they said I should only expect to be hurt by his carelessness.

Instead, I gave in to a man they never expected to be able to love me wholly and free.

They sure are disappointed...

OVERWHELMED, IMPOSSIBLY IN LOVE.

loved him. Deeply with a strength I guess I'd preserved especially for him because I'd never used it before for any reason. Until him. He came along and my heart began to realize that I'd squandered away all of the love and passion I'd been gifted and this time I'd better not waste any. I started loving him almost immediately. He came into my life and I knew that I could give him the love I'd saved up for no one. It was just lying there dormant.

I wasn't waiting for anyone to spend it on. I wasn't looking hoping or wishing for anyone. I knew the love was there but I'd tucked it away somewhere. I thought I'd never find it again. Never expecting to love or be loved again. But then he came. Not in any magical fairy tale way. But he just sort of showed up and never stopped. I noticed him first. I spoke first. But I did not love first.

The first month and then another and another until almost twelve had gone by before I acknowledged that he loved me. Two more months whizzed by and I finally acknowledged that I loved him too. It took two more weeks after that for me to say it out loud. To verbalize my feelings in a way he could understand. But when I did, it was like no time had passed at all. Rather, it felt like we'd just met. Like we'd just began our journey together.

Those words, the simple, "I love you," started life over for us again. We were the same but we weren't.

Once you've learned to love, you change. Once you learn to be loved, you are never the same.

And I never was.

Everything was different. I even noticed changes in my voice, in my walk. My entire being was in love. My toes tingled when he climbed into bed beside me. My tummy fluttered when he called my name. My skin tickled under his touch. My ears came alive at the sounds of his voice. No part of me missed out on the celebration of new love. Every part of my spirit rejoiced with the promise and hope he brought along with him. I breathed in his scent, left over on unwashed sweats, and his face came to mind instantly. I could feel his touch, hear his whispers, taste his lips. One lingering scent at the washing machine brought him to me like some sort of spell.

Maybe that's what it was. I was spellbound. I was enraptured. He had taken my being captive and I prayed to never meet release. I was happy; a slave to his love. And I knew he returned the sentiment. There was no part of me now that existed without or beyond him. We had become one. One mind, one heart, one purpose, one function. To love one another.

I lost contact with any part of myself that hadn't known how to love him. I jumped in feet first, plunged myself into the cold waters of fear and sank down where my body met the warmth of his love. I loved him. I breathed him. I became him. But he loved me first and that is worth noting.

Long before I'd dipped my toe or even given in to the thought of it, he had loved me. He bled love in everything he did for me. Love lay on the tip of his tongue with every word he spoke. Doubt had no room to linger once I began to taste love on his skin and feel it seeping through his pores. Once, I even saw love radiate right off his face and I knew. I was safe in love with him. Love didn't hurt. Love wasn't confusing or hard. Love existed for him as second nature. It was in him, on him, of him. He taught me how to live in love. I dwelled in it at first only because he was there. But soon, I started to settle in. He made room for me. I planted myself inside and took up residence.

I didn't ask for permission. I snatched love from him like it was owed to me. And in a way it was. I deserved love. I was entitled to the joy and bliss of love. I grabbed it tight and held on for every bump in the road. But the bumps were so few and far between I stopped even expecting them. When we hit them, I'd go flying but he always caught me, got me back down to earth where I couldn't forget him. We lived together in love. Just us two.

We shut out the world at times and simply basked in the delight of one another. He stared at me, I kissed him. He caressed me and I let laughter escape. He'd let a tear fall and I'd catch it on my pinky. I wanted nothing more than to keep him from pain but our little love nest was only so protective. We had to deal with the real world. But we never let life get in the way. I kept him quiet, safe. He kept me strong and sane. I fought for him he followed up with quick jabs to anything in our way. I loved him from the tippies of my toes and he loved me even more.

He became a light, I became a compass. We neither led nor followed. We simply were and just are. I loved him so deeply I got lost. Over and over again, he found me just to lose himself in me.

He   loved   me.   Deeply.   And   still.

ACKNOWLEDGEMENTS

To God … I thank you for the gift of words, art and creativity. I thank you for the courage to write, to give and to share.

To Michele … you have been the greatest support system a daughter could ever ask for. I am the woman and the writer I am because of your love and sacrifice. I write because you made me believe in my own voice.

To my friends … DeMario, Rabin, Jasmine, Tiera, HerBrina, Danielle, Brittany, Monisa, Darrell, Aieshia, Kia ... and there are so, so many more of you ... I love you all. Thank you for supporting me, for reading my work, allowing me to vent and always blowing my head up!

To Suzanne, your editing has done wonders. What could I have done without your gift?

If you are reading … I wrote this for you. Because I believe in the power and strength of love. Because I believe in the sanctuary of writing. Because
I know that someone else needs my words more than I do. Because I wasn't given this gift just to keep it all to myself.

Thank you.

I love you all,

M. Lauren

ABOUT M. LAUREN

M. Lauren is a voraciously verbose poet, novelist and blogger. In 2016, she founded the web magazine for women of color: *My Melanin Rocks!* where she writes about love, femininity and blackness. In addition, M. Lauren has written for *FlyPaper Magazine, Kingsrowe, Polished Cleveland* and her own personal blog, *And Looking?*.

Iceland-born and Cleveland-bred, M. Lauren can be found binge watching dry comedy, running from her moody attack cat or fantasizing about Chadwick Boseman.

You can catch up with M. Lauren at:

mymelaninrocks.com

mlauren@mymelaninrocks.com

Twitter: @emellewriter @mymelrocks_mag

IG: @emellewriter @mymelaninrocks

Made in the USA
Columbia, SC
14 June 2018